OUR PeRFECT MARRIAGE

ADJECTIVE

A JOURNAL FOR SWEET NOTHINGS, ROMANTIC MEMORIES,
AND EVERY FIGHT YOU'LL EVER HAVE

Alan and Claire Linic

QUIRK BOOKS

PHILADELPHIA

DEDICATION

To Oboe Linic. Thank you for all of the kisses, buddy.
Who's a good boy? Who's a good boy?

ACKNOWLEDGMENTS

LAUREN MACLEOD
A lit agent star
More rare than Halley's Comet
Come to lift us up

BLAIR THORNBURGH
Sent red pen edits
Nerd warrior of our dreams
Kisses and kisses

Copyright © 2016 by Alan Linic and Claire Linic
All rights reserved. Except as authorized under U.S. copyright law,
no part of this book may be reproduced in any form without written
permission from the publisher.
Library of Congress Cataloging in Publication Number: 2016930949

ISBN: 978-1-59474-934-6
Printed in China
Typeset in Coronet, Sackers Gothic, and Chronicle
Designed by Timothy O'Donnell
with Molly Rose Murphy
Cover photo © Cigdem Simsek / Alamy Stock Photo
Production management by John J. McGurk

QUIRK BOOKS
215 Church Street
Philadelphia, PA 19106
quirkbooks.com

10 9 8 7 6 5 4 3 2 1

Table of Contents

INTRODUCTION

5

HOW TO USE THIS BOOK

7

CHAPTER ONE

Getting to Know Each Other

9

CHAPTER FOUR

Us Out and About

91

CHAPTER TWO

Our Perfect Wedding

41

CHAPTER FIVE

Us at Home

109

CHAPTER THREE

Our Milestones

69

CHAPTER SIX

Looking Forward

127

PROOF THAT WE ARE QUALIFIED TO WRITE THIS BOOK

Marriage License

STATE OF INDIANA   MARION COUNTY

TO ANY REGULAR MINISTER OF THE GOSPEL OF ANY DENOMINATION, JEWISH RABBI MORE THAN EIGHTEEN (18) YEARS OF AGE HAVING THE
CARE OF SOULS, JUSTICE OF PEACE OF SAID COUNTY, JUDGE OR CHANCELLOR, THE GOVERNOR, THE SPEAKER
OF THE STATE SENATE OR THE SPEAKER OF THE HOUSE OF REPRESENTATIVES—

Greeting: You or either of you are hereby authorized to solemnize

The Rite of Matrimony

Between   Alan   C.   Linic

and   Claire   L.   Meyer

according to the Statutes of the State of Indiana in such case made and provided. Provided always, that the license be issued
under the hand of the Clerk of the County Court of the county where the female resides or be issued by the Clerk of the County
Court of the county where the marriage is solemnized; otherwise these shall be null and void, and shall not be accounted any
license or authority to you or either of you, for the purpose aforesaid, more than though the same had never been prayed
or granted, etc.

Given at the Clerk's Office of said County, this 17th day of December 19 48

Don Boley

COUNTY COURT CLERK

D. C.

Introduction

CONGRATULATIONS, YOU CRAZY KIDS.

You have embarked on the grand adventure of marriage—the most trying and allegedly rewarding milestone in the human experience, short of having a baby. You put on rings. You said the vows. You made your parents cry because the wedding was "not what they expected." And now you have *Our Perfect Marriage* (unless you're reading someone else's copy, in which case please stop being a cheap weirdo and buy your own). Consider this book a blank canvas upon which to paint your marital masterpiece—well, it's not *technically* blank, but you know what we're saying.

Now for some real talk: just like marriage, filling out this book is work. Both of you will make sacrifices to become something greater than an individual. There will be tears, there will be confusion, and there will be many breaks for seven-hour Netflix and cuddle sessions. But somewhere along the way, there will come the *magic*—the ineffable and inevitable result of taking two people and fusing them into a single unit, like Jeff Goldblum and the fly in the 1986 romantic comedy *The Fly*. Unity and self-knowledge are a big deal, and they come from the disasters just as much as from the accomplishments. Don't hold back.

This book helps you remember every moment and milestone of your marriage that transformed "you and me" into *we*. The finished project should be just as unique and wonderful as the couple who made it together. There will be instructions along the way, but feel free to ignore them. Who are we, anyway? Literally no one knows.

We love you and good luck.

[signatures]

P.S. Sorry we said "I love you" so soon. We're just excited about where this is going. Don't make it weird.

Super Writer

award is presented to

For

Claire

signed _____ Date: _____

GOOD WRITER
CERTIFICATE

PRESENTED TO

Alan

English Teacher

The directions: Follow them! Or if you have a better idea,
do that instead. We're not the boss of you.

KEEP IT PRIVATE. Privacy begets honesty, and honesty is the wellspring of truth, and truth is the cornerstone of trust, and trust is essential if you are ever going to commit a major crime together. The only people who should see the inside of this book are you, and maybe the federal prosecutor if it's subpoenaed into evidence. Keep this book out of sight of guests, children, and pets. If your guests tend to be nosy, keep this book in a medicine cabinet filled with marbles so that you can hear them trying to snoop.

SKIP AROUND! Maybe open the book to a random page every couple of days and see what sounds like fun to do. You can do it forward, you can do it backward, you can do it upside down . . . *if* you know what we mean.

SKIP A PAGE! Not all marriages are alike, so if a section or page doesn't apply to you, feel free to paint an impressionist landscape over it. It's as simple as that.

WRITE NEATLY, YOU SLOBS! It'll make it easier for your snooping guests to read.

DO IT TOGETHER! The book is about the two of you, and it's something to do as a couple. For maximum togetherness, we recommend sitting on each other's laps and/or writing with your arms linked like you're drinking champagne.

BE DETAILED! Love is in the little things, and hopefully this book will give you a place to record some of those little things so it'll be easier to wax nostalgic about them later or use them in a fight.

CHAPTER ONE

Getting to Know Each Other

I used to rush into things a lot. That didn't work too well.
Now I take it slow—get to know the girl and stuff. I found that it works better.
But if it's really awesome, I'll jump into it.
—NICK JONAS

Getting to Know Each Other

Before there was we there was you and me.
So who is who in this book?

ME

PLEASE PRINT

SIGN HERE   DATE

YOU

PLEASE PRINT

SIGN HERE   DATE

NOTE: By signing your names, you guarantee that you will invite us to all
your future dinner parties as well as pay for our subscription to any current
or future magazine with Ellen DeGeneres on the cover.

Meeting Me

Date of Birth: ....

Height: ....

Weight (in pounds): ....

Signature Scent: ....

Celebrity Doppelgänger: ....

LOL no, really: ....

Star Sign: ....

First Pet: ....

Favorite Planet: ....

Karaoke Song: ....

Life Goal: ....

....

....

STUNNING PHOTO

EXTRA CREDIT

Biggest Accomplishment: ....

....

....

....

Meeting You

Date of Birth: ....

Height: ....

Weight (in kilograms): ....

Allergies: ....

Blood Type *(circle one)*:   A   B   AB   ABBA   O+   O-

SSN: ....

Average Grade in Gym: ....

Plastic Surgeries: ....

Deepest Regret*: ....

....

....

....

....

DECENT PHOTO

EXTRA CREDIT:

The One That Got Away: ....

....

....

....

* NOTE: Regrets can be expanded upon in more painstaking, excruciating detail by stapling additional pages to the back of this questionnaire.

All about Me According to You

FORGERY OF MY SIGNATURE:

ENDORSE CHECK HERE

X _____

DO NOT WRITE, STAMP, OR SIGN BELOW THIS LINE

**Age when you think
I lost my virginity:**

....

MY FAVORITE CANDY:

....

(*Did I eat some
immediately after
losing virginity?*) ☐ YES ☐ NO

?

**MY FAVORITE
MOVIE(S):**

....

....

**Did I like
Titanic?** ☐ YES ☐ NO
(*the film*)

**Did I like
Titanic?** ☐̶ ̶Y̶E̶S̶ ☐ NO!
(*the ill-fated
ocean liner that
sank tragically in
the Atlantic?*)

MY MOST ANNOYING HABIT:

....

....

....

MY FAVORITE
FOOD: ....

MY FAVORITE
DRINK: ....

My Favorite Position (*sexual or otherwise*):

....

Draw my
spirit animal:

MY FAVORITE COLOR

14

All about You According to Me

Let Me fill out this page about You! Don't worry about it; just do your best.

MY FAVORITE
FOOD:

MY FAVORITE
DRINK:

I tend to thoughtfully leave our car's gas tank at:

F   E

MY FAVORITE BOOK(S):

Exes I'm Still in Contact With:

STEREOTYPE I FIT MOST:

- [ ] Hooker with a heart of gold
- [ ] Chatty hairdresser
- [ ] Scheming politician
- [ ] Plucky intern
- [ ] Antagonistic mail carrier
- [ ] Kindly grandparent
- [ ] Other:

My Net Worth:

$ ☐☐☐ , ☐☐☐ , ☐☐☐ . ☐☐

WORDS I PRONOUNCE WRONG:

MY FAVORITE COLOR

Draw my profile picture:

Did I like *The Godfather*?

- [ ] YES
- [ ] *YOU BROKE MY HEART!*

FOR OFFICE USE ONLY

Record Date _____

Initials _____

All about Me According to You

MY MORNING ROUTINE:

THE TIME I SET MY ALARM FOR IS:

THE TIME I ACTUALLY GET OUT OF BED IS:

MY LAUGH SOUNDS LIKE:

How I Feel About Children: (*circle one*):

OMG ADORBS   HEH! CUTE!   PLEASE PUT THAT DOWN   ?#@*&%!   ...   DEATH, TAKE MY HAND

My Worst Dinner Party Story:

Describe the way I eat:

Me finds this manner of eating:

☐ Endearing

☐ Fascinating from an anthropological standpoint

☐ A good appetite suppressant

All about You According to Me

Good luck, Me!
These are some real zingers.

MY FIRST KISS WAS (*check all that apply*):

☐ Sweet   ☐ Awkward

☐ Captured on a Jumbotron   ☐ Illegal in some states

Other: ....

EXISTENTIAL QUESTIONS THAT
KEEP ME UP AT NIGHT:

....

....

....

★★★ MAKE QUESTIONNAIRES GREAT AGAIN ★★★

Indefensible Political Views:

....

....

....

Draw the worst present
I've ever given you:

5

**THINGS I CAN'T
LIVE WITHOUT:**

....

....

....

....

....

I smell like:

....

....

17

Our Annoying Habits

ME

1	Do you bite your nails?	☐ YES ☐ NO
2	Do you talk with food in your mouth?	☐ YES ☐ NO
3	Do you pee in the shower?	☐ YES ☐ NO
4	Do you leave clothes in the dryer for 24 hours plus?	☐ YES ☐ NO
5	Do you believe in aliens?	☐ YES ☐ NO
6	Do you keep library books past their due date?	☐ YES ☐ NO
7	Do you secretly think you might be a vampire?	☐ YES ☐ NO
8	Do you dress as your favorite politician for fancy dinners?	☐ YES ☐ NO
9	Do you think this makes me look fat?	☐ YES ☐ NO
10	Do you find these questions annoying?	☐ YES ☐ NO

YOU

1	Do you hog the remote?	☐ YES ☐ NO
2	Do you leave dishes in the sink for 24 hours plus?	☐ YES ☐ NO
3	Do you still talk about high school?	☐ YES ☐ NO
4	Do you know every line of more than two movies?	☐ YES ☐ NO
5	Do you smell people's hair when you meet them?	☐ YES ☐ NO
6	Do you often wish you were a squirrel?	☐ YES ☐ NO
7	Do you stand outside Bruce Springsteen's house every night?	☐ YES ☐ NO
8	Do you like to dance to slow jazz in the bathroom?	☐ YES ☐ NO
9	Do you wish you had George Washington's hair?	☐ YES ☐ NO
10	Do you want to be doing something else?	☐ YES ☐ NO

Inside Our Minds

Marriage requires psychological compatibility. Are the two of you made for each other or doomed for failure? Only inkblot tests will tell!

①

WHAT ME SEES:

....

WHAT YOU SEES:

....

②

WHAT ME SEES:

....

WHAT YOU SEES:

....

ANSWER KEY **1** Trees in a windstorm. **2** Your mother, scolding you. **3** A uterus. Obviously! I mean look, at it: there's those little tube things, there's some ovaries or whatever . . . Look, we're not doctors. But both of *us* saw a uterus. **4** Two wolves ballroom dancing. No? Well, have it your way, *Crazy*. Let's move on. **5** You didn't see a badger doing a handstand? Okay, we gotta stop. You're both nuts. Official diagnosis.

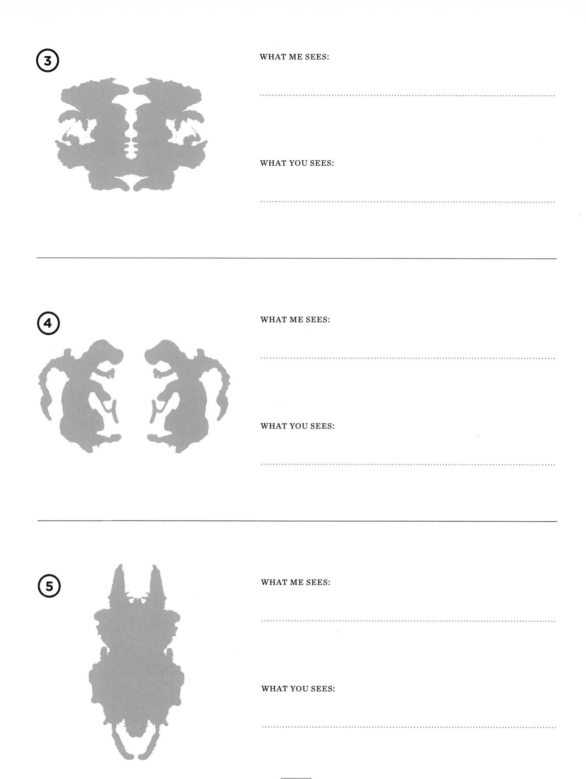

③

WHAT ME SEES:

....

WHAT YOU SEES:

....

④

WHAT ME SEES:

....

WHAT YOU SEES:

....

⑤

WHAT ME SEES:

....

WHAT YOU SEES:

....

A Full Set of Fingerprints

Me	LEAVE THIS SPACE BLANK	TYPE OR PRINT LAST NAME FIRST NAME MIDDLE NAME		SEX	RACE
				HT (inches)	WT
		CONTRIBUTOR AND ADDRESS	ALIASES	HAIR	EYES
				DATE OF BIRTH	
SIGNATURE OF PERSON FINGERPRINTED				PLACE OF BIRTH	

YOUR NUMBER	LEAVE THIS SPACE BLANK
SCARS AND MARKS	CLASS. _____
PLACE **FBI NUMBER** HERE	
SIGNATURE OF OFFICIAL TAKING FINGERPRINTS DATE	REF. _____
☐ CHECK IF NO REPLY IS DESIRED	

RIGHT HAND

1. Thumb	2. Index Finger	3. Middle Finger	4. Ring Finger	5. Little Finger

LEFT HAND

6. Thumb	7. Index Finger	8. Middle Finger	9. Ring Finger	10. Little Finger

Classified .... Assembled	Note Amputations	Prisoner's Signature
Searched .... Verified		
Index Card .... Answered		

Four Fingers Taken Simultaneously			Four Fingers Taken Simultaneously
Left Hand	L. Thumb	R. Thumb	**Right Hand**

	LEAVE THIS SPACE BLANK	TYPE OR PRINT			SEX	RACE
You		LAST NAME FIRST NAME MIDDLE NAME			HT (inches)	WT

CONTRIBUTOR AND ADDRESS   ALIASES

HAIR   EYES

DATE OF BIRTH

SIGNATURE OF PERSON FINGERPRINTED

PLACE OF BIRTH

YOUR NUMBER

LEAVE THIS SPACE BLANK

SCARS AND MARKS

CLASS. _____

PLACE **FBI NUMBER** HERE

REF. _____

SIGNATURE OF OFFICIAL TAKING FINGERPRINTS   DATE

☐ CHECK IF NO REPLY IS DESIRED

RIGHT HAND

1. Thumb	2. Index Finger	3. Middle Finger	4. Ring Finger	5. Little Finger

LEFT HAND

6. Thumb	7. Index Finger	8. Middle Finger	9. Ring Finger	10. Little Finger

Classified .... Assembled ....

Searched .... Verified ....

Index Card .... Answered ....

Note Amputations

Prisoner's Signature

Four Fingers Taken Simultaneously		Four Fingers Taken Simultaneously
Left Hand	L. Thumb / R. Thumb	**Right Hand**

Our Normal Hand-Holding Formation

Roll clasped hands in ink.
Press firmly below:

COMMON CLASP TYPES
AND THEIR MEANINGS:

**DOWNWARD-FACING
PALM**
*Me feels concerned,
protective of You*

THE "RELAXED LACE"
*You and Me's relationship is
built on mutual trust*

THE "IRON FIST"
*Me will punch supermarket
cashier in the throat if they
smile at You*

DNA Samples

Lick below.

Me

Gene Simmons

You

How We Met as Me Remembers It

One day, ... decided to go to .... in order to do
　　　　　　YOU'S NAME　　　　　　　　　　　　　　PLACE WHERE WE MET

.... In a twist of fate, ... had also decided to go to
IMPORTANT TASK　　　　　　　　　　　　ME'S NAME

....
PLACE WHERE WE MET

When .... and .... saw each other at
　　　　ME'S NAME　　　　　　　　　YOU'S NAME

.... they knew something had gone very right. ....
PLACE WE MET　　　　　　　　　　　　　　　　　　　　　　　　　　ME'S NAME

started a conversation, and that conversation ended with a lot of promise about

what was to come.

For days after their meeting, ... couldn't stop thinking about
　　　　　　　　　　　　　　　ME'S NAME

.... felt the same way. They found reasons to hang
YOU'S NAME　　　YOU'S NAME

out again at places like .... and .... It didn't take long for
　　　　　　　　A COOL PLACE　　　　　ANOTHER COOL PLACE

them both to realize that they .... each other. That's why they're
　　　　　　　　　　　　　　　VERB ENDING IN -ED

still together to this day—and to think it all started at ....! They lived
　　　　　　　　　　　　　　　　　　　　　　　　　PLACE WHERE WE MET

.... ever after.
ADVERB

How We Met as You Remembers It

One day, a dashing young hero named .... met someone new named

M">YOU'S NAME

.... was overall a wonderful person, but our

ME'S NAME   ME'S NAME

hero could tell that this would be no ordinary open-and-shut case of heroism. No

matter how much time .... heroically invested, it seemed that

YOU'S NAME

.... always needed a little something more. Soon, all ....

ME'S NAME   YOU'S NAME

thought about was how to give .... a .... that would

ME'S NAME   NOUN

truly last. That's when it finally dawned on .... What ....

YOU'S NAME   ME'S NAME

needed wasn't wasn't a hero at all. It was a ....

NOUN

   With heroic and monumental fortitude, ... made huge sacrifices—

YOU'S NAME

.... stopped ...., said goodbye to .... ,

ADVERB   BAD HABIT ENDING IN -ING   CRAPPY EX-FRIEND OF YOU'S

and even quit doing .... to make sure that time was spent instead

STUPID FORMER HOBBY OF YOU'S

being the .... that .... needed. And in this way,

NOUN   ME'S NAME

.... became an even .... hero than ever, all the time, and

YOU'S NAME   ADJECTIVE

.... better recognize.

ME'S NAME

Animal Instincts

FOR ME:

Draw an animal, real or made-up, that
you feel represents your partner.

Draw an animal, real or made-up,
that you feel represents you.

Which animal would you rather
keep as a pet?

Do you really think you're ready
for that kind of responsibility?

Animal Instincts

FOR YOU:

Draw an animal, real or made-up,
that you feel represents your partner.

Draw an animal, real or made-up,
that you feel represents you.

Which animal would win in a fight?

What do you think that says about
your marriage?

Charting Us

OUR FAVORITE FOODS

YOUR

MY

OUR

OUR FAVORITE MOVIES

YOUR

MY

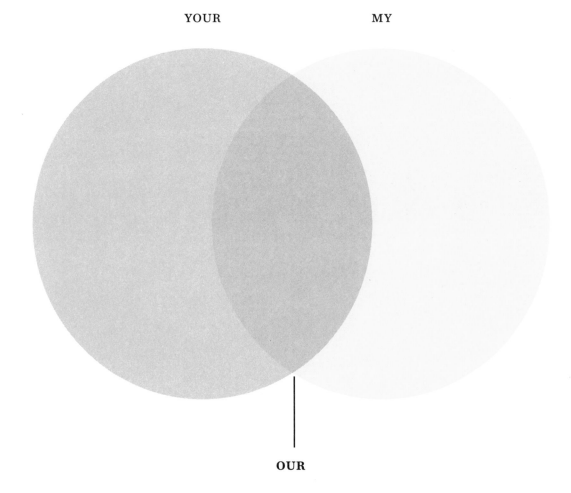

OUR

What Percentage of the Pants in This Marriage Is Worn by Each of Us?

KEY	
▪	**Me**
▫	You

The Feelings Matrix

Plot the following aspects of your relationship on the chart according to where they fall on the feelings axes.

- Our time together
- Our time apart
- Our finances
- Our sex life

- Our living situation
- Our relationship with Me's parents
- Our relationship with You's parents
- Our pets or children

NOTE Please do not play Battleship™ on the matrix.

Battleship is a registered trademark of the Milton Bradley Corporation.

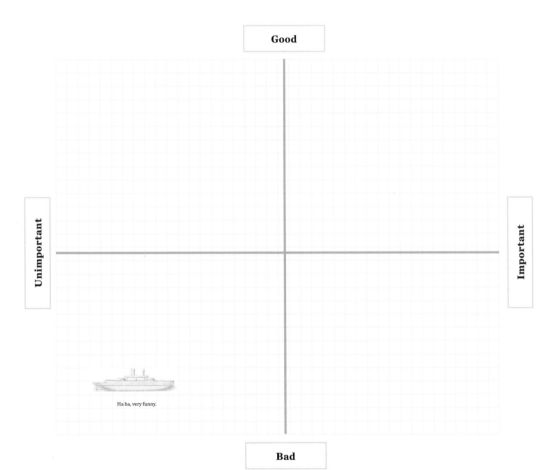

Good

Unimportant

Important

Ha ha, very funny.

Bad

Home Sweet Home!

OUR ADDRESS IS:

STREET

CITY   STATE   ZIP +4

THE CASH/JEWERLY/FINE SILVER IS LOCATED:

PLEASE DON'T HURT US

We keep the thermostat at:

O

☐ Fahrenheit
☐ Gesundheit
☐ Celsius

THE TRICK TO
GETTING THE SHOWER
TO WORK IS:

We:
(check one)

☐ RENT
☐ OWN
☐ INHERITED FROM
A DOWAGER AUNT
☐ SQUAT

How many square feet is our home?

☐☐,☐☐☐
sq. ft.

OUR FAVORITE THING ABOUT OUR HOME IS:

Our place smells like

unless *someone* forgot to take out
the trash again.

—

Just for the record, our trash day is:

M   T   W   Th   F   S   S

—

Just for the record, *someone's* name is:

Our WiFi password is:

Our neighbor's WiFi password is:

OUR SECURITY CODE IS:

1 OFF	2 AWAY	3 STAY
4 MAX	5 TEST	6 BYPASS
7 INSTANT	8 CODE	9 CHIME
# READY	0	*

Here's a photo of the
building we live in:

Here is a rendering of our home's
floor plan by a licensed architect:

What Watt?
Indicate the various
wattage light bulbs you
prefer for each room:

Living Room ....

Dining Room ....

Bathroom ....

Bedroom ....

Kitchen ....

Attic ....

Our Family Crest

Only a few hundred years ago, it was almost impossible to find a divorced couple unless you hung out at King Henry VIII's house. These days, the number of couples whose marriages end in divorce is approaching almost 50 percent. Seen together, these two facts are what a statistician would call "absolute proof" that the death of the family coat of arms is directly responsible for the dissolution of the modern marriage. Guarantee the longevity of your new family by creating your brand new insignia with these simple questions.

① WHAT IS THE MOST COMMON PHRASE USED IN OUR HOUSEHOLD?

....

....

TIP	For added class, translate your slogan into Latin. Here are some helpful terms:	Uxor .... *Spouse* Ignis .... *Fire* Potens .... *Powerful* Temptatio.. *Temptation*	Mors .... *Death* Numquam ...... *Never* Semper......... *Always* Carpe diem...... *YOLO*

② WHAT'S YOU'S FAVORITE ANIMAL?

....

③ PUT A MOOD RING ON ME. WHAT COLOR IS IT?

....

④ WHAT'S THE OFFICIAL FLOWER OF THE STATE/TOWN/COUNTRY WHERE WE MET?

....

⑤ WHAT COLOR ARE YOU'S EYES?

....

⑥ WHAT'S A TOOL OR INSTRUMENT ME USES AT THEIR JOB?

....

....

⑦ WHAT'S THE COLOR OF THE ROOM WE ARE CURRENTLY IN?

....

Time to design!

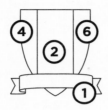

Write your new family credo in the banner at the bottom of your coat of arms. Next, draw the animal from question 2 into the bottom portion of the crest. Then draw the flower from question 4 and the object from question 6 into the upper left and upper right portions of the crest. Use the colors from questions 3, 5, and 7 to fill in the background of each third of the crest.

CHAPTER TWO

Our Perfect Wedding

Love is the master key that opens the gates of happiness,
of hatred, of jealousy, and, most easily of all, the gate of fear.
—OLIVER WENDELL HOLMES, SR.

Marriage means *hello* and *goodbye*.

Hello

to a new life.

Hello

to checking in every couple of hours.

Hello

to "I don't know—should we have sex tonight?"

Goodbye

to peeing with the door closed.

Goodbye

to first-date kisses.

Goodbye

to being alone. *Especially when you pee.*

Last Known Pre-Engagement Photos of Us

Place photos here:

Wow, you look really happy here.

A More Than Decent Proposal

The wedding day is to a marriage as the birth is to a baby: it's the day for the calendar. It's the one we celebrate as the origin and the one for which we pass gifts around each year in sheer shock and joy that it somehow still exists. But the proposal is to a marriage as the conception is to a baby: the true beginning. The moment of change. The fun part.

HOW WAS IT PLANNED?

....

....

....

....

....

WHAT WAS ME WEARING?

....

....

....

....

WHAT WAS YOU WEARING?

....

....

....

....

Where were we at the time?

....

....

THE RECIPIENT'S RESPONSE:

☐ YES! (bursts into tears)

☐ NO! (bursts into laughter)

☐ (shrug)

☐ (spit-take)

THE PROPOSAL TOOK PLACE AT:

☐ A.M.

☐ P.M.

☐ I DO NOT KNOW WHAT THIS NUMBERED CIRCLE IS SUPPOSED TO REPRESENT (see below)

THE PROPOSAL TOOK PLACE AT:

88:88 AM PM

Which knee was gotten down upon?
(*if applicable*):

- ☐ LEFT
- ☐ RIGHT
- ☐ BOTH

How nervous was the proposer?

- ☐ VERY
- ☐ SOMEWHAT
- ☐ COOL AS A CUCUMBER

WHO GOT THE FIRST
ENGAGEMENT CALL?

At a rough estimate to be confirmed by a jeweler later, the ring was how many carats?

WHAT WAS GOING THROUGH ME'S MIND?

IF IN PUBLIC, DID IT CREATE AN AWKWARD SCENE AMONG PASSERSBY? DESCRIBE.

DID WE GET ANY FREE STUFF FROM THE RESTAURANT/BAR/CASINO/ PET SUPPLY STORE WHERE IT ALL HAPPENED?

Our social media announcement was:

Wedding Planning Fights Checklist

The best part of planning a wedding is all those juicy fights
you get to have along the way. What did you two fight about?
Check all that apply.

Venue	DJ
Seating chart	Invitation design
Budget	Save-the-date design
Menu	Thank-you card design
Bachelor/bachelorette party	Hotel for us
Photographs	Hotel for everybody else
Rehearsal stuff	Hotel for dogs
Date	Budget again
Honeymoon	Type of cake
Something old	Inviting exes
Something new	Whose idea this was
Something borrowed	Eloping instead
Something blue	Spending all of this damn money
Something else	on a house instead
Wardrobe	Your aunt is not singing
Officiant	Having a prayer or not
Vows	Picking a reading
Weather	Is marriage even realistic in
Prenuptial agreements	today's society?
Whether to have a gift registry	If they don't RSVP, they can't eat
Where to have a gift registry	This whole thing is out of control
What to put on the gift registry	What were we thinking?

Together Forever with ~~Rick Astley~~ You

Place your best and/or funniest
wedding photo here.

Wedding Day Hall of Shame

WORST DANCER:

....

WEIRDEST SMALL TALKER:

....

WORST MOMENT:

....

....

....

Awkwardest Single-Friend Hookup:

[   ] **+** [   ] **(+** [   ] **)**

in case of threesome

BIGGEST COMPLAINER:

....

THING WE WISH WE COULD UNDO:

....

WORST DRESSED:

....

Thing We Forgot:

....

....

....

....

....

DRUNKEST GUEST:

GUESTS WHO ARRIVED LATE:

GUESTS WHO DIDN'T RSVP BUT SHOWED UP

And Therefore Will Never Deserve Thank-You Notes:

News from the Day We Were Married

Paste clippings below.

The *New York Times*:

The *Onion*:

The *Chicago Tribune*:

TMZ:

The Weather Channel:

Our hometown paper:

Twitter trending topics:

That one wingnut friend's
Facebook status:

Craigslist:

Picture Perfect

A portait of You the day We were married,
as drawn by Me.

A portait of Me the day We were married,
as drawn by You.

Director's Cut: The Wedding That Almost Was

Just like a romance movie, a wedding is a story about two people coming together, surrounded by a world of friends, family, obstacles, gifts, and too-crazy-to-be-real moments. Also like a romance movie, the people "in charge" of a wedding often don't get final say on the end product before it gets pushed out in front of an audience. It's time now to reflect on the wedding that You and Me really wanted . . . but that We did not.

PEOPLE THAT ME WANTED AT THE WEDDING BUT DIDN'T INVITE BECAUSE OF YOU:

....

....

....

....

Food/entertainment that Me would have loved to have if You allowed *fun* at the wedding:

....

....

....

....

Me (☐ DID / ☐ DID NOT) want to perform the Chicken Dance

COLOR SCHEME THAT ME HAD THAT YOU SHOT DOWN (TAPE SWATCHES BELOW):

The cake design that Me wanted (draw in frosting below):

PEOPLE THAT YOU WANTED AT THE WEDDING BUT DIDN'T INVITE BECAUSE OF ME:

....

....

....

....

....

Food/entertainment that You would have loved to have if Me allowed *fun* at the wedding:

....

....

....

....

....

You $\left(\begin{array}{l} \square \text{ DID} \\ \square \text{ DID NOT} \end{array}\right)$ want to mash cake into Me's face

FLORAL ARRANGEMENT IDEAS THAT YOU HAD THAT ME SHOT DOWN (PRESS FLOWERS HERE):

The venue that You wanted (sketch below):

THINGS WE AGREE TO DO DIFFERENTLY NEXT TIME AROUND:

....

....

....

....

Let's Try This Again: More Truthful Vows

ME'S VOWS

I promise never to make fun of you when you .... Or mention that

VERB

time that you .... in (*choose one*) bed/my parents' house/church.

VERB ENDING IN -ED

Even if you decide to keep .... as a hobby, I will still love

VERB FOR SOMETHING STUPID ENDING IN -ING

you. I will support your love of eating .... I solemnly swear to always

DISGUSTING FOOD

close the door when I .... as long as you promise to try to stop

SHAMEFUL VERB

.... at the dinner table. I'll always be there to listen when you want

SEVERELY IMPOLITE VERB

to talk about .... I'll be a shoulder to cry on while you watch

THAT ONE BORING THING YOU LIKE

.... I promise always to love you, and we'll live

TEAR-INDUCING TELEVISION SHOW AND/OR COMMERCIAL

.... ever after.

ADVERB

I promise not to laugh when you .... I'll try really hard to forget

VERB

the time that you .... in (*choose one*) school/work/my cousin's Bar

EMBARRASSING VERB ENDING IN -ED

Mitzvah. I will support your love of .... but will organize

STUPID WASTE-OF-TIME THING

an intervention if it gets any worse. I'll breathe through my mouth when you're

cooking .... because you know how much I hate the way it (*choose*

NASTY HOMEMADE FOOD

one) smells/tastes/looks .... I will lessen how often I sing along to

SHAMEFUL ADVERB

.... though I will never stop forever because I think you secretly love

HIT SONG OF THE '80s, '90s, OR TODAY

it. I'll be here when you want to complain about...

TERRIBLE COWORKER'S NAME

I won't tell anyone how much .... makes you cry, but I will be there

TEARJERKING MOVIE AND/OR SONG

when it does. I'll always be around when you need a partner in ....

CRIMINAL AND/OR HOBBY ACTIVITY

And we'll live .... ever after.

ADVERB

Who Got What

Some photos of our big haul!

Me's absolute favorite wedding present:

You's absolute favorite wedding present:

Something We didn't ask for but
are *super* thankful that we got:

The gift We knew we're returning pretty much right away:

We aren't sure who this gift was from:

Doubles! Something We got twice or already own:

No, Thank You

Traditional wedding etiquette dictates that a couple should send thank-you notes between two weeks and two months after the wedding. We say to hell with tradition; everyone will get their notes when we're good and ready. To make this terrible tradition slightly more bearable, use these handy photocopiable templates.

To someone you actually care about (parents/ grandparents/family dog)

DEAR _____,

WE ALREADY SPOKE ABOUT THIS IN PERSON.

LOVE,

_____ & _____

To someone who *clearly* cheaped out on the gift

Dear _____,

New phone. Who is this?

Love,

_____ & _____

To someone who gave you . . . something? Damn. Look through the registry. Was it the crock pot?

Dear _____,

Your gift was truly a gift to us. We use your gift just as much as you would expect someone to use this gift. The gift looks great in the room it was designed to be in. This gift made us too emotional to speak of, so please—never ask us about it in person.

Vaguely,

_____ & _____

To the coworker who wasn't actually invited but showed up anyway because he/she saw it on Facebook

DEAR _____,

I PEED ON SOMETHING IN YOUR DESK THAT YOU USE DAILY.

LOVE,

_____ & _____

To someone you're pretty sure attended the wedding

Dear _____,

Thank you so much for your support of our union. Your presence was certainly felt. We noticed you didn't send a gift and have written our return address in bold on the envelope.

Love always,

_____ & _____

Our Song

Whether it's the song that played during your first dance, on your first date, or at the conclusion of the ceremony, every couple has a song. It doesn't even matter what it is—it only matters what it means. Use this helpful answer key to translate the true meaning behind your couple anthem.

OUR SONG IS:

BY:

Answer Key	
SONG LYRIC	**TRANSLATION**
"love"	*tolerate*
"never dreamed that"	*totally figured that*
"you"	*anyone from your particular background, really*
"someone like you"	*probably like a hundred of you scattered around the world*
"forever"	*like, a really long time and stuff*
"your eyes"	*sex things*

OUR SONG'S LYRICS:

VERSE 1:

....

....

....

....

CHORUS:

....

....

....

....

VERSE 2:

....

....

....

....

WHAT THEY ACTUALLY MEAN:

VERSE 1:

....

....

....

....

CHORUS:

....

....

....

....

VERSE 2:

....

....

....

....

Proof! Suckers!

Place your marriage certificate below.
If you cannot find your marriage certificate,
forge one.

Would We Do It Again?

<table>
<tr><td>⌇ ME ⌇</td><td>⌇ YOU ⌇</td><td>If both of you answered *Yes,* continue on to Chapter Three.</td></tr>
</table>

ME	YOU	
☐ YES	☐ YES	If both of you answered *Yes,* continue on to Chapter Three.
☐ NO	☐ NO	If one or both of you answered *No* or
☐ MAYBE	☐ MAYBE	*Maybe,* briefly express your deep disappointment in your partner below:

....

....

....

....

....

....

....

....

....

....

....

IN LOVING MEMORY.

"ME
TIME"

Our Milestones

First comes love, then comes marriage,
Then comes marriage counseling.

How Long Have We Been Married?

WE HAVE BEEN MARRIED SINCE

...., ... at .... o'clock A.M./P.M.

MONTH   DAY   YEAR

That was .... years, ... months, ... weeks, ... days,

.... hours, and .... minutes ago. Time flies!

We Lasted Longer Than
(check all that apply)

☐ Britney Spears & Jason Allen Alexander: *55 hours*
☐ Carmen Electra & Dennis Rodman: *9 days*
☐ Kim Kardashian & Kris Humphries: *72 days*
☐ King Henry VIII & Anne of Cleves: *184 days*
☐ Robert Redford & Lola Van Wagenen: *9,855 days*

OUR NEXT ANNIVERSARY WILL BE THE .... **ANNIVERSARY** *(choose from below)*

1st year	*Paper*	10th year	*Back rub*
2nd year	*Cotton*	15th year	*Omaha Steaks™*
3rd year	*Leather*	20th year	*Meteorite*
4th year	*Flowers*	25th year	*Taxidermied animal*
5th year	*Rayon*	30th year	*Porridge*
6th year	*Candy*	35th year	*Signature scent*
7th year	*Limestone*	40th year	*Foot rub*
8th year	*PVC pipe*	45th year	*Organ donation*
9th year	*Vinyl*	50th year	*You've given enough, don't you think?*

The Story of Us as Told by Receipts

Tape receipts below. If you didn't keep your
receipts, draw them. If you don't remember
the purchases, make them up.

FIRST GROCERY TRIP:

FIRST RESTAURANT:

FIRST HUGE SPENDING MISTAKE:

FOUND THIS ONE IN A POCKET, NO IDEA:

Our First Haircut

Paste photos here.

ME BEFORE

YOU BEFORE

ME AFTER

YOU AFTER

Hair Keepsake

Each partner should tape a lock of their hair here. It's like olden times, except fancier.

TIP If one or both of you is bald, substitute leg, armpit, or toe hair.

DANDRUFF SUFFERER?
Shake your hair over the winter landscape below, like Ally Sheedy did in *The Breakfast Club*.

Me's hair:

You's hair:

The First Time One of Us Got Sick

No one ever realizes how serious (and sometimes gross) the "in sickness and in health" part of the vows can be until the first time someone is really ill. But taking care of each other is part of the gig, and the first time is a milestone to remember.

Who got sick? ☐ YOU ☐ ME   **What was wrong? Check all that apply:**

Nausea	Sleep problems
Fever	Lycanthropy
Chills	Itchiness
Cough	Sensitive teeth
Barfing	Fuzz butt
Dog breath	Rumble tummy
Bunions	Cravings
Excessive sass	Mood swings
Hallucinations	Amnesia
Stomach pain	Phone hand
Wobble body	Repetitive or compulsive behavior
Runny nose	Repetitive or compulsive behavior
Runny eyes	Repetitive or compulsive behavior
Runny nipples	Couch slouch
Poopy stuff	Fashion disaster

☐ YOU ☐ ME **did the following as caretaker:**

Made soup	☐ YES ☐ NO	Went to the drugstore begrudgingly	☐ YES ☐ NO
Took the sick one's temperature	☐ YES ☐ NO	Went to the drugstore gladly	☐ YES ☐ NO
Muttered "There, there"	☐ YES ☐ NO	Made inappropriate jokes about finding a replacement spouse	☐ YES ☐ NO
Pressed a cool cloth to the sick one's fevered brow	☐ YES ☐ NO	Jack-all	☐ YES ☐ NO

THE WORST PART:

....

....

....

....

....

....

....

Unflattering photo
of the Sick One!

Our First Big Married Trip

Our first time traveling together (not counting the honeymoon) was for:

☐ Vacation
☐ Business
☐ Holiday

We went to:

WHAT WE DID:

....

....

....

....

....

....

....

EXCHANGE RATE AT THE TIME OF TRAVEL:

....

WE RATED THE TRIP: (*circle one*)

| Me | 1 | 2 | 3 | 4 | 5 |
| You | 1 | 2 | 3 | 4 | 5 |

BIGGEST RIP-OFF:

....

....

WHO WE SAW:

....

....

....

SCARIEST MOMENT:

....

....

....

WHAT WE ATE:

....

....

....

We got there by:

☐ TRAIN
☐ PLANE
☐ AUTOMOBILE
☐ BUS
☐ CRUISE SHIP
☐ HELICOPTER
☐ HOVERCRAFT

Visa stamps

**Tape a photo or two
from the trip here.**

Hopefully one in which one
person is giving the other bunny
ears. If you do not have a photo
in which one person is giving the
other bunny ears, please return
to the location and take one
before proceeding. Bunny ear
photos are *comedy gold*.

Big Questions

The joy of being married is always having someone to talk to. The terror of being married is that your spouse has already heard everything you have to say. But no couple forgets those landmark conversations which establish that you and your partner are truly compatible. Use the following questions as a jumping-off point for one such talk. Record any relevant notes on the right hand page.

What's the most important thing in a relationship? What are the sexiest qualities a partner can have? What constitutes cheating? How should a couple share finances? How should we celebrate Valentine's Day? What is the government hiding from us? Why have humans gotten taller through the ages? How do ghosts travel, and why? Is edible soap sexy or gross? What's the difference between snakes and tailless lizards? Who is best: Picard, Kirk, or Dumbledore? Would Jerry Seinfeld be funnier if he was two feet tall? Are Lunchables a valid food source? Magnets. How do they work? What is to be done about the slow yet imminent commercialization of Hanukkah? Which of our friends could we rely on in a zombie apocalypse? What's the exact moment that Monopoly transitions from being the best to the absolute worst board game of all time? Like, when *exactly* does that happen? Is Cash4Gold a drug front or just a regular scam? Either way, what are they doing with all that gold? What kind of animal would make the best Earth Overlord?

Big Answers?

The First Time Me Messed Up

Boy, howdy, today .... really goofed it. We both know there is one
_____ ME'S NAME

rule in ...., and it's that you ....
_____ HOUSE'S NICKNAME   _____ EMPHATIC ADVERB   _____ DO OR DON'T

.... Man, when .... realized that ....
_____ THING THAT WAS DONE   _____ YOU'S NAME   _____ ME'S NAME

had broken that rule, some blood got to boiling. .... got so
_____ YOU'S NAME

.... that .... just had to apologize. ....!
_____ EMOTION   _____ ME'S NAME   _____ VENTING CUSSWORD!

How hard is it to remember to simply .... ? Clearly too hard
_____ ACTION THAT WOULD HAVE AVOIDED A FIGHT

for .... to remember, or maybe .... just
_____ ME'S NAME   _____ ME'S NAME

.... Sometimes it feels like we're doing this on purpose, just
_____ OTHER POTENTIAL REASON FOR SCREWUP

poking and prodding at each other until the end of time for the sheer schadenfreudal

glimmer of joy that comes from making each other go .... insane. Is
_____ ADVERB

this what we signed up for? Is this what marriage is? The answer is ....
_____ WRITE "YES" HERE

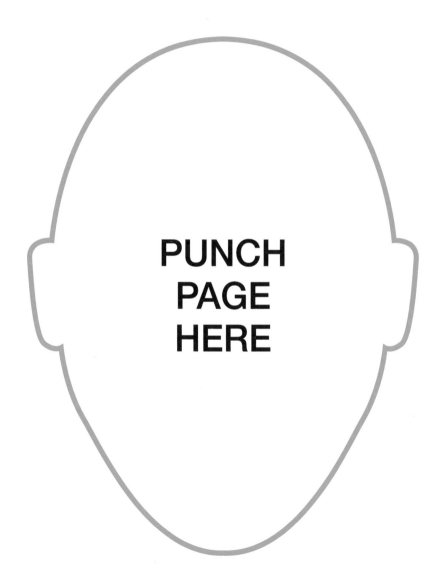

PUNCH
PAGE
HERE

The First Time You Messed Up

Well, well, well. Looks like we're not all perfect, eh, ...? Because

<small>YOU'S NAME</small>

if there's one thing you know, it's that .... needs to be done a certain

<small>TASK YOU MESSED UP</small>

way. But .... walked into .... and guess what? The

<small>ME'S NAME</small>   <small>LOCATION OF MESS UP</small>

.... ended up all kinds of .... We all best believe

<small>TASK / OBJECT / AREA</small>   <small>FAVORITE SYNONYM FOR "MESSED UP"</small>

that .... is gonna squeeze about .... apologies out of

<small>ME'S NAME</small>   <small>TRIPLE DIGIT NUMBER</small>

............................'s .... Hoo boy, we all can't wait to see how

<small>YOU'S NAME</small>   <small>BODY PART APOLOGIES SHOULDN'T COME FROM</small>

.... is going to react to this when .... posts this whole

<small>MUTUAL ACQUAINTANCE</small>   <small>ME'S NAME</small>

thing to ....

<small>SOCIAL MEDIA OF CHOICE</small>

Moving-On Method for Me

STARE
SMUGLY
HERE

STILL NOT READY TO FORGIVE?

Stare at this picture for about 20 seconds and then look at a white surface. An image of Jesus telling you that you could have done better will appear.

Whose Fault Is It Anyway?

Who is generally responsible for all the fights?
Fill out these simple graphs to determine the answer.

Me's Chart

KEY
INSTIGATOR:
☐ You
☐ Me

You's Chart

The Post-Fight Mantra

You can't always agree on everything, and recovering from a disagreement can be hard. But rest assured that even the happiest couples throughout history had their fair share of fights. The Munsters fought. Bonnie and Clyde fought. Even Donny and Marie fought, and they weren't even married. When you're having trouble getting over a spat, just read this page aloud to your loved one.

......................................, I am angry about our fight.
PARTNER'S NAME

The molten rage of a thousand dying suns is pouring through my veins and

threatening to erupt from my eyes with all the viciousness of a rabid laser weasel.

I am not telling you this just to share my feelings, ...
AFFECTIONATE NICKNAME FOR PARTNER

I am telling you this so that you know to be afraid.

Because we live in the same place and I have the power to make home decorating

purchases that will bring your whole world crumbling down. I hope you like

......................................, sucker!
FURNISHING OR DECOR ITEM PARTNER DOES NOT LIKE

Less Popular Milestones

Anything can be a milestone if you want it to be!
Fill in the dates and any relevant notes below.

WE MADE A LEAF PILE.

.... / .... / ....

WE FOUGHT IN PUBLIC.

.... / .... / ....

WE WENT TO A WEDDING TOGETHER.

.... / .... / ....

WE LATER AGREED OUR WEDDING
WAS BETTER.

.... / .... / ....

WE BAKED TOGETHER.

.... / .... / ....

WE GOT BAKED TOGETHER.

.... / .... / ....

WE FORGOT AN ANNIVERSARY.

.... / .... / ....

WE GAVE EACH OTHER NEW PET NAMES.

.... / .... / ....

WE SAW A TERRIBLE MOVIE.

.... / .... / ....

WE MADE A SEXUAL MISTAKE.

.... / .... / ....

Babies! The Cutest Milestone

If you haven't already had babies, the whole world is wondering . . .

When are you having babies?!?

- ☐ SOON
- ☐ SOONISH
- ☐ WHEN WE GET AROUND TO PUTTING SOME OF THOSE PLASTIC THINGS IN ALL THE OUTLETS
- ☐ NEVER

IF YOU HAVEN'T HAD BABIES AND YOU ARE TIRED OF PEOPLE ASKING . . .

. . . play the Baby Card, literally! Photocopy this useful card to carry in your wallet.

Baby Card

WE WILL HAVE AS MANY BABIES AS WE WANT <u>WHEN</u> WE WANT.

(That may mean no babies, ever.)

If we do have a baby, we may even allow it to be a musician. Get outta our business, fools!

IF YOU'VE ALREADY HAD A BABY . . .

. . . nice. Draw a heart below for every baby you have, proportional to how much you love it.

IF YOU ARE ONE OF THOSE COUPLES WHO REFER TO YOUR PETS AS "FUR BABIES" . . .

. . . that is weird. Maybe don't?

A Photo of Our Baby

If you do not have an actual baby, substitute a photo of a pet, a car, a plant, or a weird sock pile you drew eyes on. Whatever you invest your time and love into!

CHAPTER FOUR

Us Out and About

It doesn't matter where we go.
All that matters is that we get the hell outta here.

The Date Log

Does Me like dates?
☐ YES
☐ NO

What about You?
☐ YES
☐ NO

Someplace we will never go again:

SOME OF OUR RECURRING DATE SPOTS:

....

....

....

....

....

....

....

The exact number of dates we have been on is:

....

HOW MUCH DO WE SPEND ON A TYPICAL DATE?
☐ $0–25 ☐ $25–50 ☐ $50–100 ☐ $100+

DO WE USUALLY GET OUR MONEY'S WORTH?
☐ YES ☐ NO ☐ Trick question—you can't put a price on TOGETHERNESS!!!

ME'S FAVORITE DATE PLACE:

....

....

....

YOU'S FAVORITE DATE PLACE:

....

....

....

Fill in this pie chart to show the different types of dates we go on

KEY	
☐ DINNER	☐ ICE- AND/OR ROLLER- SKATING
☐ MOVIES	☐ COUPLES' COUNSELING
☐ DANCING	
☐ BRUNCH	☐ OTHER
☐ PIE CHARTING	

The Amazing Unique Date Generator

Are you bored with your current dating routine? Well, maybe you should be. But never fear—you've got options! Without peeking at the table below, each of you should pick a number between 1 and 10.

BASED ON ME'S NUMBER:	BASED ON YOU'S NUMBER:
1. Double Date	1. Dinner
2. Blindfold	2. Movie
3. Handcuffed	3. Putt-putt
4. Reverse	4. Ice-skating
5. Underwater	5. Live show
6. Imaginary	6. Picnic
7. Long-distance	7. Bowling
8. Russian	8. Museum
9. Puppet	9. Racing
10. Infinite	10. CPR course

Hi! Welcome to the upside-down part! Use Me's number to pick a modifier from the first column, then use You's number to pick a "classic" date idea from the second column. Put them together for a brand-new take on an old favorite! You can thank us later.

WELL DONE! WRITE YOUR NEW DATE-TIVITY HERE:

Double Dating

WE LIKE TO DOUBLE DATE WITH THESE COUPLES:

....

....

Is that because we feel our relationship is better than theirs? ☐ YES

WE DO NOT LIKE TO DOUBLE DATE WITH THESE COUPLES:

....

....

Is that because one of them is weird? ☐ SORT OF

Or because both of them are weird? ☐ YEAH, IT'S PRETTY ROUGH

OUR SAFE DOUBLE DATE SPOT:

....

....

....

OUR SECRET SIGNAL THAT IT'S TIME TO GO:

....

....

....

OUR GENTLE REJECTION TO FUTURE DOUBLE DATE PROPOSITIONS:

....

....

....

OUR GO-TO "LET'S WRAP THIS UP" EXCUSE:

....

....

....

OUR FAVORITE THIRD WHEEL ....

Keeping the Love Alive on Date Night

Having troubles keeping date night spicy? Let us help you out.

Buy flowers. Go to a candlelit restaurant. Go to a candlelit restaurant and use the candle to set the tablecloth on fire. To get nice and tender for date night, marinate yourselves in Worcestershire sauce before going out. Skype from two different locations to experience twice as many date activities at once. Drink a whole bottle of wine. Drink a bottle of wine, whole. Like, just swallow that sucker. Break into an ATM. Buy a dog. Actually, don't buy. Adopt. But don't adopt unless you are ready. Animals are not a gift. Animals are a life commitment. If you can't commit to a dog, then don't adopt. Your place doesn't really have that big of a yard anyway. Y'know what? Finish your own damn list.

Celebs We Can Bang

ME	YOU
1.	1.
2.	2.
3.	3.
4.	4.
5.	5.

THE RULES: This list expires .... years from today, at which time it may be revised in cases of celebrity death, religious conversion, or early-onset ugliness. Each party must agree upon the other's list. Neither party can choose Olympic athletes. That's not fair to the rest of us.

Expiration date: ....

Number of revisions allowed: ....

Are we joking ☐ YES
about this? ☐ NO

ME'S SIGNATURE   DATE

YOU'S SIGNATURE   DATE

SWORN AND SUBSCRIBED TO before me this .... day of ...., ...

My commission expires: ....

....
NOTARY PUBLIC

A Very .... !
ADJECTIVE   HOLIDAY

Add photos here:

Our Grocery List

We love food! Here are all the things we usually buy (check all that apply)

Bread	Dog and/or cat food
Eggs	Magazines
Milk (regular)	Tin foil
Milk (soy)	Four $50 Applebee's gift cards
Milk (some other weird kind)	Candy
Cereal	A premade birthday cake with
Bananas	hilariously ugly decorations
Butter	Bagels
Soda pop	Squagels
Laundry detergent	Kegels
Ricotta cheese	Kale
Shredded cabbage	Fresh flowers
Apple cider vinegar	It's just that some people buy their
Gummy vitamins	spouses flowers once in a while, is all
Ping-pong balls	Never mind
6 for $6 Krunchtastic™ Store- Brand Potato Chips	One of those little eyeglasses repair kits from the checkout

Brand Matters!

When it comes to ...., Me always wants to get ....,
FOOD PRODUCT   BRAND NAME

but You grew up with .... and pitches a fit if We don't buy it.
OTHER BRAND NAME

WHY ME'S BRAND IS BETTER:

....

....

....

....

....

....

WHY YOU'S BRAND IS BETTER:

....

....

....

....

....

....

NOTE: If the two of you cannot reach an agreement while filling out this page, then you must fight about it loudly in the dairy aisle during your next couple's grocery trip.

Our Hunnies' Moneys

Who says financial planning can't be romantic
and also make people fight a lot?

| The Chief Financial Manager of the house is: | ☐ ME ☐ YOU | The Deputy Financial Manager of the house is: | ☐ THE OTHER ONE |

Together, we make $ ☐☐☐,☐☐☐* **a year.**

OUR MORTGAGE/RENT/BLACKMAIL COSTS ARE:

$ ☐,☐☐☐,☐☐☐

OUR STUDENT LOAN DEBT IS:

$ ☐☐☐,☐☐☐,☐☐☐.☐☐

We **will** / **will not** (*circle one*) pay it off
before we die.

YOU'S BAD SPENDING HABITS:

....

....

....

ME'S BAD SPENDING HABITS:

....

....

....

✱ NOT ENOUGH BOXES? If you earn in excess of $999,999 per year, please refer
(rather, command your manservant to refer) to the Millionaire's Edition of *Our
Perfect Marriage*, available wherever good books are sold for $85,000.

Who Gets What, Just in Case

You've heard about prenups. You've heard about postnups. But what about the midnup?
Yes, just because you're somewhere in the middle of your marriage doesn't mean you
can't decide who technically owns which assets, including pets.
Write down who gets what in the blanks below.

TV	☐ YOU	☐ ME	Books	☐ YOU	☐ ME
Movies	☐ YOU	☐ ME	Music	☐ YOU	☐ ME
Furniture	☐ YOU	☐ ME	Vehicles	☐ YOU	☐ ME
Pets	☐ YOU	☐ ME	Home	☐ YOU	☐ ME
Bank accounts	☐ YOU	☐ ME	Clothes (all of them)	☐ YOU	☐ ME
Jewelry	☐ YOU	☐ ME	Food	☐ YOU	☐ ME
Hygiene stuff	☐ YOU	☐ ME	Social media passwords	☐ YOU	☐ ME

ME'S SIGNATURE   DATE

YOU'S SIGNATURE   DATE

We at Work

Me, the Provider

JOB TITLE

COMPANY

SALARY

DUTIES:

....

....

....

BEST PART OF THE JOB:

....

....

....

WORST PART OF THE JOB:

....

....

....

A TYPICAL DAY AT WORK GOES LIKE:

....

....

....

THE DREAM JOB I AM WORKING TOWARD IS:

....

....

....

My office spouse is named: ....

How does You feel about this "office spouse"? ☺ ☹

You, the Breadwinner

CURRENT POSITION

EMPLOYER

SALARY

RESPONSIBILITIES:

....

....

....

HIGH POINT OF THE JOB:

....

....

....

LOW POINT OF THE JOB:

....

....

....

A TYPICAL DAY AT WORK GOES LIKE:

....

....

....

THE DREAM JOB I AM WORKING TOWARD IS:

....

....

....

CUBICLE/DESK DECORATIONS:
- ☐ Plants
- ☐ Action figures
- ☐ One of those drinky birds
- ☐ A mug with a funny saying
- ☐ Photos of Me
- ☐ No photos of Me?!
- ☐ What about that cute one from last summer?
- ☐ Fine.

We around the World

Where have We been?

Mark the locations according to what We did there:

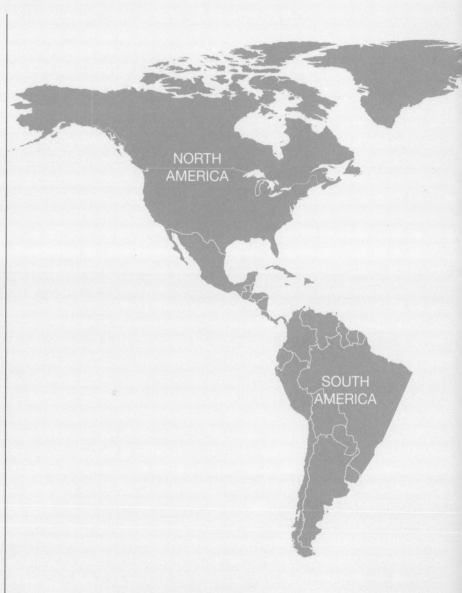

☺ LIKED IT!

☹ HATED IT!

🤢 GOT FOOD POISONING

☀ GOT SUNBURNED

💲 GOT WALLET STOLEN

? SOME DISAGREEMENT OVER WHETHER WE ACTUALLY WENT HERE OR NOT

Our bucket list of places to go:

....

....

....

....

....

....

NORTH AMERICA

SOUTH AMERICA

Getting Away from Each Other

Spending time apart is vital to ensuring that the time you spend together is healthy and happy. This is confirmed by science, which says that 100 percent of people who do not get alone time will die at some point during their lifetime. Don't be foolish! Escape your spouse *for your own health*.

Me needs	You needs
.... HOURS alone time per week.	.... HOURS alone time per week.

ALONE ACTIVITIES THAT ME PREFERS:

....

....

ALONE ACTIVITIES THAT YOU PREFERS:

....

....

THINGS ME ENJOYS THAT YOU HATES TO DO:

....

....

THINGS YOU ENJOYS THAT ME HATES TO DO:

....

....

ACTIVITIES WE PREFER TO DO TOGETHER:

....

....

THINGS WE BOTH HATE TO DO BUT SOMEHOW END UP DOING, LIKE, ALL THE TIME:

....

....

The Great Escape!

Often, the bathroom is the only place where you have any hope for some alone time (assuming you lock and/or barricade the door). Try to beat your spouse to that tiled sanctuary for some well-deserved stare-into-the-middle-distance time.

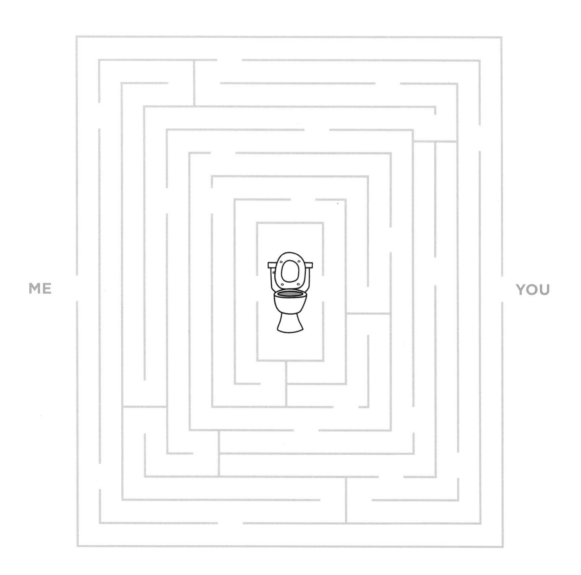

CHAPTER FIVE

Us at Home

Home: the one place you can't escape each other.
—ANCIENT MATRIMONIAL PROVERB

The Morning Routine

FOR ME:

Me's alarm goes off at .... : ....

Me hits snooze .... times.

Me gets up for real at .... : ....

Me ....

Me ....

Me ....

Me packs ....

Me leaves the house at .... : ....

Is Me a morning person?

☐ YES
☐ CoffeeCoffeeCoffeeCoffee CoffeeCoffeeCoffeeCoffee

FOR YOU:

You's alarm goes off at .... : ....

You hits snooze .... times.

You gets up for real at .... : ....

You .... me.

You ....

You ....

You leaves the house at .... : ....

You comes back because of a forgotten ....

Is You a morning person?

☐ (whistling cheerful tune)
☐ ~~FUCK YOU~~
The publisher apologizes for any offense caused.

The Nightly Schedule

.... arrives home.
ME OR YOU

.... does ....
PERSON ABOVE   ACTIVITY

.... arrives home.
OTHER PERSON

.... happens.
EVENT

We ....
ACTIVITY

.... cooks / orders dinner.
NAME

.... does ....
NAME   ACTIVITY

.... cleans up after dinner.
NICER SPOUSE

We ....
ACTIVITY

Then we ....
ACTIVITY

Time permitting, we may also ....
ACTIVITY

Bedtime!

PERFERRED PRE-BEDTIME BEVERAGE:
(*optional*)

☐ Sleepytime™ tea
☐ Single malt scotch
☐ Mouthful of water from the faucet and 3 Ambien

Chore Assignments

Share a life, share the joy, share the work! You know your current chore "system" is hideously flawed to nonexistent, so sort it out here: flip a coin, and let whoever wins the toss get first pick of one chore from the list below. Then take turns choosing a chore until the least desirable one is left. Just like picking teams in middle school gym class!

Take out the trash	☐ YOU ☐ ME		Clean the kitchen	☐ YOU ☐ ME
Sort the recycling	☐ YOU ☐ ME		Tidy dining room	☐ YOU ☐ ME
Vacuum/ sweep floor	☐ YOU ☐ ME		Clean windows/ mirrors	☐ YOU ☐ ME
Clean the bathroom	☐ YOU ☐ ME		Consume leftovers	☐ YOU ☐ ME
Re-clean bathroom properly	☐ YOU ☐ ME		Seasonal decorating	☐ YOU ☐ ME
Tidy living room	☐ YOU ☐ ME		Organize books/ movies/music/games	☐ YOU ☐ ME
Tidy bedroom	☐ YOU ☐ ME		Trophy polishing	☐ YOU ☐ ME
Do the laundry	☐ YOU ☐ ME		Handymanning	☐ YOU ☐ ME
Sort the mail	☐ YOU ☐ ME		Couch warming	☐ YOU ☐ ME
Go grocery shopping	☐ YOU ☐ ME		Watch TV and make cleaning suggestions	☐ YOU ☐ ME

All that's left now is to keep each other on task. Organize your choices into the proper columns and decide on a frequency for them. For example, something like dishes might need to be done once every two days, whereas trophy polishing should probably happen twice a day to achieve maximum shine.

ME'S CHORES	FREQUENCY	YOU'S CHORES	FREQUENCY

The Territory Map

It may be *our* house, but there's still gotta be some "me space." Choose a color to represent Me and another to represent You. For some of the major areas of your home, use those colors to show who has claimed what space.

COLOR KEY

◯ YOU

◯ ME

BOOKSHELF

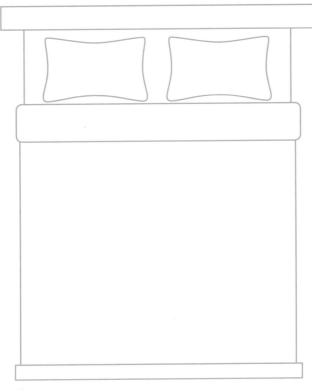

BED (BIRD'S-EYE VIEW*)

TRASH CAN

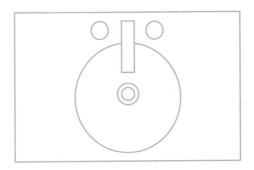

BATHROOM COUNTER

* In other words, some bird has been watching you have sex.

Making Our House a Home

A checklist of the things you need to be
truly happy in your own space.

Elaborate name for your home, like "Pemberley" or "Elsinore"	Oil portraits of dead relatives
	Stone gargoyles
Personalized door knocker	Stone Phillips
Ornate, cushy carpets	An emotionless butler
Silver gravy boat	Creaking floorboards
Silver butter dish	Self-playing piano
A fancy sitting robe	A rolling fog that never dissipates
Oak bookcases	Secret passageways
Velvet curtains	Wrench
An in-house bar	Ballroom
A suit of armor	Ghosts
Chandelier	Inexplicable blood stains
Grand staircase	*My God, is that a human hand??!*

Movie Night!

Title: ....

Genre: .... Rating: ....

Plot summary: ....

....

....

....

Who picked it? ☐ YOU ☐ ME   *Did we like it?* ☐ YES ☐ NO

Title: ....

Genre: .... Rating: ....

Plot summary: ....

....

....

....

Who picked it? ☐ YOU ☐ ME   *Did we like it?* ☐ YES ☐ NO

Title: ....

Genre: .... Rating: ....

Plot summary: ....

....

....

....

Who picked it? ☐ YOU ☐ ME   *Did we like it?* ☐ YES ☐ NO

Title: ....

Genre: .... Rating: ....

Plot summary: ....

....

....

....

Who picked it? ☐ YOU ☐ ME   *Did we like it?* ☐ YES ☐ NO

Movie snacks We like?

☐ POPCORN
☐ JUNIOR MINTS
☐ NACHOS
☐ A HEALTHY BATCH OF KALE CHIPS
☐ BOURBON

WHO PICKS GOOD MOVIES?

■ YOU ■ ME

The movie character Me reminds You of:

The movie character You reminds Me of:

Weekend Warriors

How do You, Me, and We spend our weekends? List the things
We are always saying We're gonna do but We just don't:

YOU'S OVEROPTIMISTIC
IDEAS FOR THE WEEKEND

ME'S OVEROPTIMISTIC
IDEAS FOR THE WEEKEND

WE'S OVEROPTIMISTIC
IDEAS FOR THE WEEKEND

Craft Night!

A couple who crafts together has tacky decor together. Make your own personal nightmare with just a doily and some glue, and then attach your photos below.

Feeling lost?
Here are a few fun and affordable crafting tips!

PILE THINGS
IN A
MASON JAR.

**Glue something
—— to ——
something else.**

"PERSONALIZE"
HOUSEHOLD
OBJECTS BY
"MONOGRAMMING"
YOUR INITIALS
ON THEM WITH A
SWITCHBLADE OR
SHARPENED
LETTER OPENER.

START A SCARF?

---

*Forget all this and
go to the movies.*

Add photos here:

Recipes for Love

Whether it's just putting tuna from a can onto bread or spending hours slaving over a beautiful beef Wellington, making food for each other matters. Immortalize your best recipes here, and refer to this page in case of hunger-onset crankiness.

YOU'S RECIPE CARD

Recipe:...

Ingredients:..

....

Directions:..

....

....

....

....

....

....

Me's Recipe Card

Recipe:...

Ingredients:...

....

Directions:..

....

....

....

....

....

....

WE'S RECIPE CARD

Recipe:...

Ingredients:...

....

Directions:..

....

....

....

....

....

....

The Sex Stuff

Check out these sex goals and then check 'em off!

We did it in a cool new place! ☐	We definitely invented a new sex move/position/toy! ☐
We made sex for over thirty minutes! ☐	We were overheard by our neighbors! ☐
We had real spontaneous, out-of-nowhere sex! ☐	We had sex five whole times! ☐ ☐ ☐ ☐ ☐
We scheduled sex days in advance and stuck with it! ☐	We accidentally went two weeks without having sex! ☐
We used photography/video to record the sex! ☐	We deleted the photography/video! ☐ (SMART MOVE)

Sexy Suggesties

Every romantic relationship has some physical component attached to it. And sure, there are a hundred books on the topic of sex that you could read. Or you could pick a random suggestion from each category to create just-for-you sexual experiments! Our personal favorite is "chair rubbing syrup."

PLACES	OBJECTS	ACTIONS
Bathtub	Ladle	Kissing
Trunk	Wig	Licking
Hallway	Iron	Kneading
Fire Escape	Soap	Rubbing
Chair	Canary	Squeezing
Tree	Syrup	Nibbling
The Dump	A Dump	Dumping

SOME OF OUR "COMBOS TO REMEMBER":

PLACES	OBJECTS	ACTIONS

Question and Answer Sex-ion

**DESCRIBE ME DURING SEXY TIME USING
...A COMMERCIAL SLOGAN:**

....

....

....

...A PROVERB:

....

....

....

...A BREAKFAST CEREAL:

....

....

....

ME'S LEAST FAVORITE PART OF SEXY TIME:

....

....

....

A SONG ME LIKES TO SEXY TIME TO:

....

....

....

ME'S SEXIEST OUTFIT ACCORDING TO YOU:

....

....

....

Something Me
wanted to try that
We will never, ever
do again: ....

....

DESCRIBE YOU'S SEX STYLE USING ...A SONG TITLE:

....

....

....

...A BOOK TITLE:

....

....

....

...A MOVIE TITLE:

....

....

....

YOU'S FAVORITE PART OF SEX STUFF IS:

....

....

....

A MOVE YOU CAN USE TO PUT ME IN THE MOOD:

....

....

....

THE MOST ROMANTIC NIGHT YOU CAN RECALL:

....

....

....

A time You almost ruined sexy time:

....

....

CHAPTER SIX

Looking Forward

I don't like looking back. I'm always constantly looking forward.
I'm not one to sit and cry over spilt milk—I'm too busy looking for the next cow.
—GORDON RAMSAY

Looking to the Future

HOPES, DREAMS, AND GOALS FOR ME:

....

....

....

....

....

....

....

....

....

....

....

....

....

....

HOPES, DREAMS, AND GOALS FOR YOU:

....

....

....

....

....

....

....

....

....

....

....

....

....

....

Looking to the Future, Realistically

That last set you listed was really cute. No, for real! All that travel, fitspiration, and self-actualization—just great. And "Learn a new language together"? How romantic and impossible is that? Maybe you're aiming a little high is all we're saying.

Don't set yourself up for disappointment, champs. Let's take another crack at these as if we live in the real world. For example, maybe a hope for the future is "Have sex one time" or, if you're feeling gung-ho, "Do the dishes once a week."

HOPES, DREAMS, AND GOALS FOR ME:

....

....

....

....

....

HOPES, DREAMS, AND GOALS FOR YOU:

....

....

....

....

....

Time Capsule Time!

One day many years in the future, you will look back on the early years of this relationship and say to yourselves, "I can't remember a goddamn thing about it." Or you can follow this nifty guide to creating our own time capsule instead and not have to trust the fickleness of human memory!

1. **FIND A WEATHERPROOF CONTAINER,** like a chest, a plastic bin, or a bunch of those colorful eggs people hide on Easter.

2. **WRITE A LETTER TO YOUR FUTURE SELVES.** Be sure to include:
   - *The date*
   - *How you rate your relationship*
   - *Your favorite parts of being together*
   - *The big things going on in the world right now*
   - *Your guesses for what the future will be like (future We will laugh so hard at how naive and hopeful you were)*

3. **PUT IN SOME FUN KNICKKNACKS** that are descriptive of your relationship or current era. For example:
   - *A newspaper*
   - *Whatever the current currency is*
   - *A cutting-edge piece of technology, like one of your smartphones*
   - *A sample of your young blood (for cloning purposes)*
   - *Clean drinking water ("Holy shit, honey, remember this stuff?!")*
   - *Celebrity autographs*

4. **PACK A SNACK** for your future selves to enjoy while they sift through the capsule. Like cheese, or cold cuts.

5. **DIG A HOLE** in an obscure place and bury the capsule.

6. **SET SOME KIND OF GOOGLE ALERT** or calendar reminder for thirty years from now. Be sure to include capsule coordinates!

7. **WAIT THIRTY YEARS.**

8. **RECEIVE REMINDER.**

9. **LIVE TOO FAR AWAY,** replace all your reminder technology as it becomes obsolete, or not remember what the reminder is for.

10. **LIVE OUT THE REST OF YOUR LIVES,** never digging up the capsule.

Bucking the Odds

Of course your marriage is a solid bet. We'd put money on it.* But how much are we going to win back? Figure out the odds of these likely scenarios.

We stay happily married: .... TO 1

We stay grudgingly married: .... TO 1

We have kids: .... TO 1

We have grandkids: .... TO 1

We like the grandkids better: .... TO 1

We forget a major anniversary: .... TO 1

One or both of us become reality stars: .... TO 1

One or both of us end up in prison: .... TO 1

Me dies first: .... TO 1

You dies first: .... TO 1

WINNER'S TALLY:

ME:

$

YOU:

$

*NOTE: Void where prohibited. Don't do anything stupid.

The Next Generation

Whether you're pre-pregnant, already parents, or never going to be responsible for anything larger than a cat, you should plan every last detail of any future offspring's life. Do not give them any kind of leeway or free will in determining their own identity or they will run with it. You know how cats are.

MALE NAMES

NAME	NAMED FOR (RELATIVE, CELEBRITY, ETC.)	POSSIBLE SCHOOLYARD TEASING VARIATIONS ON NAME

FEMALE NAMES

NAME	NAMED FOR (RELATIVE, CELEBRITY, ETC.)	POTENTIAL MISSPELLINGS

GENDER-NEUTRAL NAMES

NAME	NAMED FOR (RELATIVE, CELEBRITY, ETC.)	LIKELIHOOD THAT CHILD WILL SPEND HIS/HER LIFE SPELLING THIS NAME FOR PEOPLE OVER THE PHONE WHEN MAKING RESTAURANT RESERVATIONS
		1 2 3 4 5 (circle one)
		1 2 3 4 5 (circle one)
		1 2 3 4 5 (circle one)

IF WE WIN THE GENETIC LOTTERY, OUR CHILDREN WILL GET:

.... ,

.... ,

AND

....

FROM ME

.... ,

.... ,

AND

....

FROM YOU

IF OUR LUCK IS REAL BAD, OUR CHILDREN WILL GET:

.... ,

.... ,

AND

....

FROM ME

.... ,

.... ,

AND

....

FROM YOU

(1) YOU'S MIDDLE NAME: **(2) ME'S FIRST PET'S NAME:**

.... **+** ....

CONGRATULATIONS! YOUR CHILD'S PORN NAME IS:

We, The Movie

LIKELY ACADEMY AWARD NOMINATIONS FOR:

....

....

....

Mononymous singer who will perform the movie's "signature song":

(choose one)

☐ STING
☐ MADONNA
☐ SEAL
☐ BEYONCÉ
☐ ENYA
☐ BJÖRK
☐ ADELE
☐ SIA
☐ PRINCE

We will require

☐☐☐ %

of box office profits

Working title:

Genre:

Likely Rating:

| G | PG | PG-13 | R | X |

PLOT SUMMARY:

....

....

....

ELEVATOR PITCH: *(choose one from each column and talk fast)*

"Like
(HEATHERS / GONE WITH THE WIND / DEEP THROAT / BRIDGET JONES'S DIARY / MOONSTRUCK)
meets
(THE GOONIES / APOCOLYPSE NOW / TRANSFORMERS / LEGALLY BLONDE / DEATH WISH)
!"

ACTOR WHO SHOULD PLAY ME:

....

....

....

ACTOR WHO SHOULD PLAY YOU:

....

....

....

The Correct Midlife Crisis

Everyone has a midlife crisis; few do it right. Make sure your MC is one for the history books with these brainstorming questions!

WHAT RIDICULOUS PURCHASE WILL WE MAKE?

WHICH LIFE-THREATENING SPORT WILL WE TRY?

HOW WILL WE TELL OUR BOSSES WE QUIT?

WHERE WILL WE GET HAIR PLUGS (WHERE IN TOWN AND WHERE ON OUR BODY)?

WHAT WILL WE BLOW OUR ENTIRE RETIREMENT FUND ON?

WHICH CELEBRITY WILL WE ASK TO BE IN A THREESOME?

WHICH COUNTRY WILL WE HIDE FROM THE GOVERNMENT IN?

HOW MANY INTERVENTIONS WILL IT TAKE TILL WE SEE THE LIGHT?

"Will" in the *Blank*

Last Will and Testament

I, ME, an adult residing at _____, being of sound mind, declare this to be my last will and testament. I revoke all wills and codices previously made by me.

ARTICLE 1

I appoint YOU as my personal representative to handle the bequeathment of my junk. There should absolutely definitely be court supervision present, and please don't hesitate to correct my personal representative should some stuff be misread or skipped. Please play the following song throughout the rest of the reading of my last will and testament: "_____"

ARTICLE 2

I direct my personal representative to just use their best personal judgement as far as my bank accounts, credits, outstanding expenses, and stuff like that. It'd be pretty nice to divide that stuff up, but if we're in the middle of installing a new Jacuzzi in our bathroom or something, just make a call and everyone will go with it.

ARTICLE 3

I devise, bequeath, and give the following to _____ : _____
_____ .

I devise, bequeath, and give the following to _____ : _____
_____ .

I devise, bequeath, and give the following to _____ : _____
_____ .

_____ and _____ can fight it out for whatever is left.

SIGNATURE: _____ SIGNED THIS DATE: _____

𝕷𝖆𝖘𝖙 𝖂𝖎𝖑𝖑 𝖆𝖓𝖉 𝕿𝖊𝖘𝖙𝖆𝖒𝖊𝖓𝖙

I, YOU, an adult residing at _____, being of sound mind, declare this to be my last will and testament. I revoke all wills and codices previously made by me.

ARTICLE 1

I appoint ME as my personal representative to handle the bequeathment and stuff of all my things. They are hereby permitted to serve without court supervision. There is an outfit ME wears that I really like that should be worn during the division of my estate: _____. This outfit should be verified before moving on to Article 2.

ARTICLE 2

I hereby declare any outstanding debts, expenses, liens, charges, loans, or pending collections to be canceled in full at the time of my death. I can do that, right? It's already done.

ARTICLE 3

I devise, bequeath, and give the following to _____ : _____
_____ .

I devise, bequeath, and give the following to _____ : _____
_____ .

I devise, bequeath, and give the following to _____ : _____
_____ .

I devise, bequeath, and give the rest to _____ and _____ .

SIGNATURE: _____ SIGNED THIS DATE: _____

Premature Eulogizations

It's never to early to start thinking about all the personal grievances
you'll finally get to air at your spouse's funeral.

YOU'S EULOGY, WRITTEN BY ME:

....

....

....

....

....

....

....

....

....

....

....

....

....

....

....

....

ME'S EULOGY, WRITTEN BY YOU:

All the Important Passwords

Don't leave your poor widowed spouse locked out of your
Netflix account in case of your untimely death!

ME'S PASSWORDS:

E-mail:

Bank Account:

Credit Card:

Secret Credit Card:

Facebook:

Twitter:

Pinterest:

Fitness Tracker:

eBay:

XXXHotFanFiction.co.uk:

YOU'S PASSWORDS:

E-mail:

Spam-Only E-mail:

Instagram:

LinkedIn:

Phone Bill:

Internet Provider:

Insurance Portal:

HBOGo:

World of Warcraft™:

HowTallIsThatCeleb.com:

A Farewell Poem

Though we may be .... for most our years,

ADJECTIVE

We'll always .... through all our fears.

VERB

And though our .... grow longer,

ADJECTIVE   NOUNS

Our love can only grow more stronger.

We, now WE, are .... together

ADJECTIVE

As .... as the ....

ADJECTIVE   ADJECTIVE ENDING IN -EST   NOUN

Together in the .... we lie,

ABSTRACT NOUN

Until we say our last goodbye.

The .... as we complete our book,

HAPPY NOUN

The .... of the life we took,

EMOTIONAL NOUN

The .... for a husband-slash-wife,

AFFECTIONATE NOUN

The newfound .... of married life.

DELIGHTFUL NOUN

And now this little book is done,

Our marriage is a perfect one!

WE DID IT!
OR, RATHER, YOU DID IT.
(THIS THIRD PERSON THING
IS GETTING CONFUSING.)

On the reverse of this page is a Certificate
of Completion, suitable for framing. Post a
photo of yourselves posing with this certificate
(looks of smug self-satisfaction on your faces
are optional but recommended) and hashtag it

#OurPerfectMarriage

There's no contest or prizes associated with this,
but just think how your lonely, single friends will seethe
with jealousy. *Eat it, losers!*

Certificate of Completion

This Certificate Acknowledges That
(thanks in *large* part to this book)

ME

AND

YOU

OFFICIALLY HAVE A PERFECT MARRIAGE.

WE DID IT.

_____
Alan Linic

_____
Claire Linic